Vostok Road Racers

RAYMOND AINSCOE

Published in 2006 by Ilkley Racing Books
3 Mendip House Gardens Curly Hill Ilkley LS29 0DD

Copyright © Raymond Ainscoe

The right of Raymond Ainscoe to be identified as the author of this work has been asserted by him in accordance with the Copyright, Designs and Patents Act 1988. All rights reserved. No part of this publication may be reproduced, stored in a retrieval system or transmitted, in any form or by any means, electronic, mechanical, photocopying, recording or otherwise, without the prior permission of the copyright owner.

Vostok Road Racers: ISBN 0 9524802 2 0

Printed by The Amadeus Press, Cleckheaton, West Yorkshire

Front cover: Endel Kiisa on the four cylinder 350 cc Vostok, 1964 East German GP at Sachsenring.

About the authors:
Raymond Ainscoe is a contributor to numerous classic bike magazines, particularly "Classic Racer" and "Legend Bike". His previous books are "Gilera Road Racers", "Laverda", "Benelli Road Racers" and "Gilera Racers: Singles and Twins". He was the scriptwriter for the video "Great Italian GP Racers". He participated in the revived Giro d'Italia in 1990 and 1992 and enjoys classic racing and parading over public roads circuits in the Netherlands and Belgium.

Born in 1937 in Kaina on the Estonian island of Hiiumaa in the Baltic Sea, Endel Kiisa became a professional rider for the Serpukhov factory. He rode both S and Vostok machines in the USSR and in Grands Prix, and won numerous Estonian titles in the 1960s. In 2000, he was voted Estonia's motorcyclist of the twentieth century. Still an enthusiastic motorcyclist, he lives outside Tallinn with his wife, Virve, and family.

CONTENTS

Acknowledgements
Foreword by Endel Kiisa
1. Introduction
2. The S racers
3. The Jawa replicas
4. The 350 Vostok
5. The 500 Vostok
6. Postscript
Appendices:
    (1) Bibliography
    (2) The GP results
    (3) Where are they now?

ACKNOWLEDGEMENTS

Welcome to the history of the Vostok Road Racers, the third in Ilkley Racing's series of books covering marques from the Golden Era of motorcycle racing.

In writing this book, I have been fortunate enough to have been assisted by numerous enthusiasts, to all of whom I offer my thanks.

For illustrations, I must thank the doyen of photographers, Mick Woollett, who scoured his archive for shots, and my friends Doug Peel, Elwyn Roberts and Sauro Rossi.

Many of the photographs have come from the collection of Mike Jordan of Hohenstein-Ernstthal who has kindly provided pictures of the Jawa-lookalike S bikes and Vostoks at Sachsenring in the 1960s. Visit his website at "www.motorrennsportarchiv.de".

My particular appreciation goes to John Caffrey who has an unrivalled experience of racing in recent years, with considerable success, on public roads circuits behind what was the Iron Curtain, and who willingly shared his detailed knowledge of racing in the Baltic states.

I must also record my gratitude to Endel Kiisa, whose photographs and recollections of his years as a Vostok works rider have formed the foundations of this book, and who kindly agreed to write the Foreword. Thanks also to his son Marek for his hospitality when I have visited the fascinating medieval city of Tallinn on so-called research trips.

Finally, a big "thank you" to my wife Elizabeth and our children, Catherine, Edward and Eleanor, for their continuing patience as I have researched and written this book (and its predecessors).

Raymond Ainscoe
Ilkley
January 2006

FOREWORD

In the 1950s, when I began racing in Estonia as a young man, I raced ancient road bikes, usually 125 cc two stroke machines, in club races. It has to be remembered that, at that time, because of the political situation and a lack of finance, Soviet riders did not compete in the West and so I never imagined that, one day, I would ride genuine, purpose-built racing motorcycles in world championship events.

However, thanks to the S-360, built in the Serpukhov factory with the collaboration of Jawa, I was able to race in Grands Prix in the early 1960s. Then, in 1964, my team mate Sevostianov and I became celebrities of sorts when, in selected title races, we rode the four cylinder Vostok which was always the centre of attention in the paddock. And it was the 350 cc multi which I rode at the Nurburgring in 1965 when our performance led to me receiving an offer to join the mighty Honda works team. Sadly, the KGB did not approve! What might have been?

But I had no particular regrets about having to stay with the Serpukhov factory squad; after all, my family and friends were in Estonia and I was happy to continue to live in Tallinn. And my years with the S and Vostok bikes took me to race in the Netherlands, West Germany and Italy, all of which were countries which, in the days of the Soviet regime, the typical Estonian could not dream of visiting. So, when the Vostoks were pulled out of international competition at the end of 1969 and I decided to retire from the sport, I did so feeling that my career had been fulfilling.

Recently, a friend of mine in Tallinn has acquired a S-360 in working order; seeing it again brings back a host of happy memories. I hope that this book and the photographs will give you a flavour of those memories and an insight into the story of racing the S and Vostok bikes forty years ago.

Endel Kiisa
Tallinn
Estonia

Endel Kiisa, with his Ducati 748, in Tallinn recently.

Chapter One: Introduction

A preliminary confession: the book should perhaps really be entitled something along the lines of "The S, CKB and Vostok Road Racers built in Serpukhov", which is a bit of a mouthful and so the title has been truncated to something more manageable.

※※※

As the story of "Vostok Road Racers" is inextricably linked with the politics of the USSR and the Baltic states in the twentieth century, a brief history lesson is in order.

In 1920, the communist government of Russia signed peace treaties with the parliamentary republics of Estonia, Latvia and Lithuania recognising their independence in perpetuity. But the Molotov-Ribbentrop non-aggression pact of August 1939 secretly divided Eastern Europe into Soviet and Nazi spheres of influence. By August 1940 all three Baltic countries had been placed under Red Army occupation, the communists had won the "elections" and all three states had been "accepted" as republics of the USSR.

So, when Hitler's armies occupied the Baltic states in 1941, they were initially welcomed as liberators and about 250,000 Estonians, Latvians and Lithuanians joined German military units - some as volunteers, others conscripted. The other side of the coin was that there were also nationalist and communist guerrilla resistance groups which fought against the Nazis.

The Red Army re-conquered the Baltic states by the end of 1944 and a ruthless policy of Russification began. Migrant workers from Russia, Belarus and Ukraine were introduced; housing and top jobs were allocated to Russian speakers; schoolchildren were obliged to learn the Russian language; the practice of religion was restricted. Thousands of Latvians took to the woods outside Riga rather than live under the repressive Russian rule; it was not until the late 1950s that the final partisan groups were cleared from the forests surrounding Riga; thousands with nationalist sympathies were executed or deported to Siberia by the KGB.

But resentment was not a one-way street; the Russians too had their gripes. Thanks to greater industrialisation, the peoples of the Baltic countries boasted a relatively high standard of living by Soviet standards. That was particularly true of Estonia; its capital, the beautiful medieval city of Tallinn, enjoyed a steady flow of visitors, trade and investment from neighbour Finland which, as a "neutral" state during the Cold War, enjoyed a close relationship with the USSR.

However, when Soviet leader Mikhail Gorbachev began to encourage "glasnost" (openness) and "perestroika" (reconstruction) in the late 1980s, the pent-up frustrations of the Baltic peoples emerged and nationalism came to the fore with demands for self-rule.

After largely peaceful mass protests, predominantly in the respective capital cities of Vilnius, Tallinn and Riga, the declarations of independence of Lithuania, Estonia and Latvia were recognised by the Western powers and the USSR in 1991.

※※※

And what of the history of motorcycle production in the USSR?

Apart from some assembly plants and modest projects in Moscow, it was not until 1928 that motorcycle production began in earnest, when a team at the steel factory in Izhevsk designed, manufactured and tested the first Izh motorcycles, powered by vee-twins of 1,200 cc. (Izhevsk is the capital of the republic of Udmurtia, with a population of about 600,000. It is a noted engineering centre, where Mikhail Kalashnikov designed his famous AK-47 assault rifle.)

The original Izhevsk-based team, under the direction of P. V. Mozharov, soon moved to Leningrad to design a 300 cc two-stroke, called the L300. However, in 1933 the former motorcycle workshop at the Izhevsk steel plant became the site of the Izhevsk motorcycle works to put the L300, re-named the Izh-7, into production. It was at Izhevsk that Vsevolod Rogozhin first entered the story; he was the chief designer at the time of the introduction of the Izh-8 (another 300 cc two stroke) which went into series manufacture in January 1938.

Another company engaged in mass production, as from 1946, was the V. A. Degtyarev plant at Kovrov in the Vladimir region. The company was founded in 1917 and produced machine guns, anti-tank guns and the like, and after the Second War it began production of the K, or Kovrovec, series of two stroke lightweight motorcycles. As from the mid-1960s, these modest motorcycles were re-badged as Voskhod, after the space programme of that name.

INTRODUCTION

The chief executive of the Serpukov bureau, Vsevolod Ragozhin, with the raised hand, at the launch of a new sidecar. He was also the USSR federation's delegate to many FIM congresses.

(The Voskhod (translated as "sunrise") space flight programme was basically a development of the manned Vostok programme, using a Voskhod craft and rocket. Voskhod One was the first space flight with more than one person on board; the crew of Voskhod Two achieved the first space walk.)

There was also a factory in Moscow which, in 1939, put into production the famous M-72, the 750 cc flat twin sidecar outfit, which had been made under licence from BMW (or which, according to some authorities, was simply an unauthorised copy of the BMW R71).

The M72 was initially built, with Stalin's nod, for military purposes and, by 1941, as Hitler's invading hordes neared Moscow, there was concern that the factory would be bombed. So it was that production was moved to a disused brewery in the town of Irbit in the Urals; the IMZ (Irbit motorcycle company) was established. After the War, production of the BMW replica continued, with the M72 being updated and achieving cult status in its Cossack and Ural versions. (Enthusiasts should contact the Cossack Owners Club.)

And what of motorcycle sport in the USSR?

The first recorded competition was a race from Moscow to Klin (a town about 30 kilometres to the north of the capital city) and back on 14 July 1918. As motorcycle production took off during the 1930s, so did competition in all its forms - road racing, moto-cross, moto-ball, enduro, speedway and ice-racing. It was on the initiative of the Soviet Motorcycling Federation that the first speedway races were held on ice, in 1936, under the auspices of the FIM.

In 1942 the Central Construction and Experimental Bureau was founded in the town of Serpukhov, about 70 kilometres from Moscow. The Bureau's purpose was to provide a research and development centre for the various mass production motorcycle factories throughout the Soviet Union.

At the end of the Second War, records and materials were brought from the DKW plant at Zschopau in eastern Germany for evaluation in Serpukhov. So it was that the Bureau began to produce a few DKW look-alike racers; the

The start and finish straight at Pirita in the 1930s

S1B, the S2B and the S3B which were unashamed copies of the 125 cc, 250 cc and 350 cc pre-War race offerings from the DKW workshops. The chief designer was engineer Ivanistky.

These early products were simply called "S" (i.e. the Russian "C") - for Serpukhov, and not for "sport", as has sometimes been written.

Both the Kovrov and the Izhevsk factories produced slightly modified versions of their road bikes for use in off-road and road race competition.

To participate in motorcycle sport, it was necessary for a would-be rider to join one of the nationwide sports clubs which were multi-disciplinary, with names such as Torpedo and Dynamo. Those names achieved renown in the West thanks to the exploits of the clubs' football sections, such as Moscow Dynamo which was the first European club to tour Britain after the War in December 1945. Some of the clubs received financial support from the state for their motorcycle competitions, with patronage from Uncle Joe Stalin who was keen on motor sports - a trait he shared with his fellow dictator Mussolini.

In the 1950s, Estonia was undoubtedly the centre of Soviet road racing, despite there being at that time no motorcycle industry in the republic.

The first Eesti Suursoit (or Estonian TT) was held on 17 September 1933 using a 6.171 kilometre course mapped out over the public roads running through a pine forest and linking the villages of Pirita, Kose and Kloostrimetsa on the outskirts of Tallinn.

The Estonian TT gained a high profile in 1937 with the entry of the formidable DKW works team, whose star rider Kurt Mansfeld won the 500 cc race. The final Eesti Suursoit, properly so-called, came in 1939 before the onset of the Soviet occupation.

However, after the war, racing resumed over the Pirita circuit and the year's principal event was in effect an unofficial USSR GP, which boasted crowds in excess of 150,000 in its heyday.

***

Finally, a word about spelling in this book. Thanks to the Cyrillic script and the Russian alphabet, and the use of different languages by the participants in the history of Vostok road racers (particularly Russian, Latvian and Estonian), the names in this story (riders, towns, manufacturers etc.) have often appeared in print in English language publications in a bewildering number of variants. Wherever possible, in this book use has been made of the spellings of names with which readers are likely to be already familiar, with apologies for any mistakes.

Chapter Two: The S Racers

Although there was motorcycle competition, and indeed record breaking, in the USSR in the immediate post-War years, there was no participation in international sport, as the governing body, confusingly called the URSS, was not affiliated to the FIM. However, by 1954 the Soviet motorcycle authorities were interested in participating on the international stage. The Central Automobile and Motor Cycle Club of Moscow applied to join the FIM in 1956, and Soviet riders and observers were invited to the Oliver's Mount road races at Scarborough - an invitation which was declined.

In readiness for international road racing, in 1954 the Serpukhov Bureau designed a new range of four stroke racers. These bikes were simply called "S" and were never entered as "Vostok" but their history is an integral part of the Serpukhov racers' tale and so a brief digression, outlining the development of the S racers, is not merely justified but essential.

125 cc

S-154
The smallest bike in the range was the single cylinder S-154. The designation (of this bike and the other S racers - with the exception of the 175 cc model) identified both the engine capacity and the year of design. Hence, "1" indicated 125 cc and "54" the year of origin.

The engine featured dohc assembly driven by a shaft (on the right hand side) and gears; it measured 54 x 54 mm for a capacity of 123 cc, and produced 12.5 bhp. The cylinder was inclined slightly forwards in a frame which was reminiscent of that of a scaled-down Featherbed Norton. Weight was about 80 kgs and top speed approximately 140 km/h.

S-154 in the Riga Motor Museum

A dustbin faired S-154, with an unidentified rider, probably at Pirita.

Records suggest that no more than four of these Ultra-lightweight racers were built in 1954 and 1955. (Some such bikes may have been dubbed as S-155 but they were probably simply those built in 1955 and not re-designed models.)

S-157
In 1957, the bike was re-designed, and the new version was duly dubbed the S-157. The cylinder, which now stood vertically, had been revised to measure 58.5 x 46 mm, which took the capacity to 124 cc and boosted power to 14.5 bhp at 10,000 rpm, with a four speed gearbox. It may well have featured a new head.

There were, apparently, ten such racers built in Serpukhov.

S-159
The final 125 cc bike, the S-159, appeared in 1959.

By then, the Serpukhov factory was liaising with Jawa to produce 250 cc and 350 cc racers (- see Chapter Three). It may be that this final Ultra-lightweight S was actually designed and built with the assistance of the Czech factory. It is to be noted that bore and stroke dimensions were 55 x 52 mm, as was the case with the S-259, the Jawa-lookalike twin cylinder 250 cc bike.

The S-159 featured a new twin plug head and a six speed gearbox. The motor now offered a reputed 21.5 bhp at 12,800 rpm and a top speed of 170 km/h. In truth, the claimed output seems to be optimistic; the Italian factories' Ultra-lightweight GP models, the twin cylinder Gilera and the MV single, were generating in the region of 18 to 20 bhp.

About eight such bikes were built in Serpukhov.

A press shot of the S-159

In addition, using drawings from the Bureau in Serpukhov, a 125 cc racer was built in Tallinn in 1958, under the control of the designer Uwe Soodla. Called "Estonia", it was reputedly faster than the S but unreliable. Indeed, some of the S racers may actually have been assembled in Tallinn, rather than in Serpukhov.

What happened to these S bikes, given that there was no official factory-based team running on a full-time basis? The bikes were sent from Serpukhov to favoured clubs in the major cities (each of which enjoyed a race workshop), there to be allocated to the best riders. The 125 cc S models (and indeed the larger capacity brethren) were far in advance of the ageing two strokes and converted road bikes available to most competitors and hence were much sought-after by ambitious pilots.

At the end of each season, the national inter-club champion was given his bike's engine as a prize, and no doubt a number of Serpukhov-built engines thereby found their way into private ownership (although in theory the factory should have ensured that all the bikes were destroyed).

The road racing highlight of the year for Soviet racers was the Pirita meeting, and for many years the annual Soviet road racing championship was decided on the results of a single meeting at Pirita - although rounds at Leningrad and Tartu (Estonia's second city) were eventually added. In 1959 Richard Laur, many times an Estonian champion of the 1950s, as chairman of the organising committee of the races, wished to revive the use of the name Eesti Suursoit (GP or TT).

But the commissars from Moscow refused to sanction the use of the tag "Estonian", fearing that it would foster potentially dangerous nationalism in what was in reality an occupied state.

Hence, although the title Suursoit was revived, the event was re-born as the Kalevi Suursoit, with Kalevi being the name of the organising club. Kalev was a legendary Estonian hero, who was said to be buried beneath Tallinn's nineteenth century, imposing Russian Orthodox cathedral - yet another symbol of the oppression of the Estonians by their grasping, aggressive neighbour. Thanks to the marketing power of the hero's brand, many Estonian institutions and products bear his name, such as Tallinn's chocolate factory and indeed the sports club, which enjoyed a car and motorcycle division.

In fact, the first Kalevi Suursoit was held in 1959 over the 8 kilometre Iru-Lukati-Kloostrimetsa public roads course but in 1960 the event returned to its spiritual home at Pirita. Leningrad's Mikhail Grigorev rode a S-154 to third place in the 1960 edition of the Suursoit. In 1961, it was switched to the Tartu public roads course and Karel Oopkamp took a S-157 to runner up spot behind Juri Randla (Ducati).

In 1962, it was back to Pirita and Enn Lossmann took the laurels with a S-157. Interestingly, the results show that Valeri Katonin and Nikolai Mikhailov retired their S-162 models. Factory records make no mention of a "162" version; presumably it was merely an updated version of the S-159.

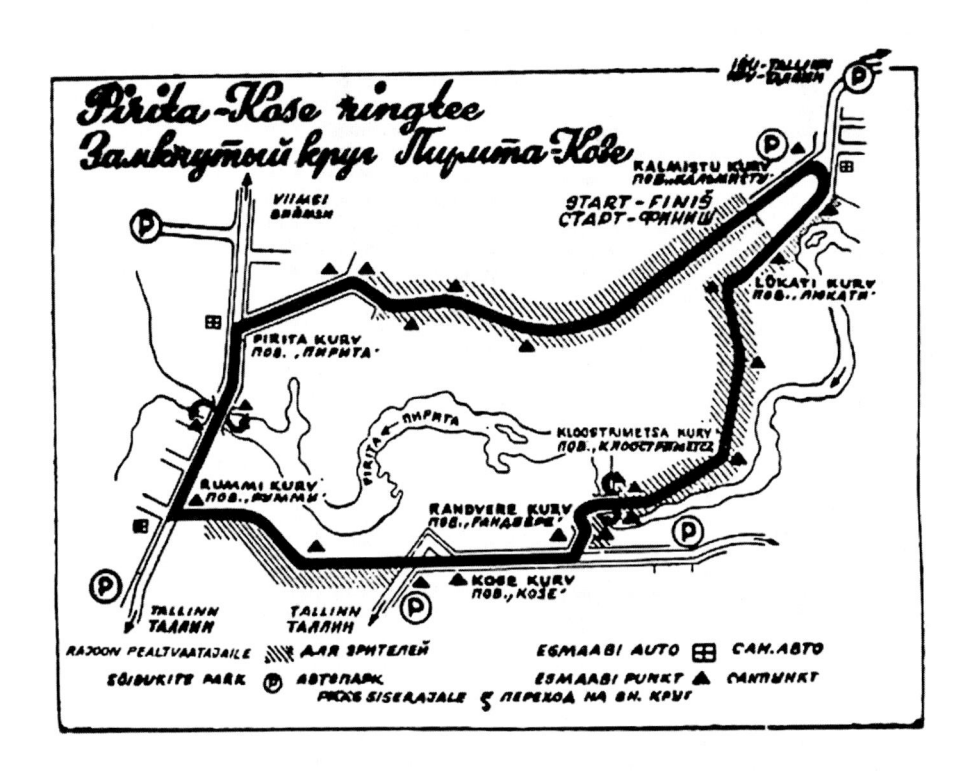

* * *

The Pirita circuit used for the Kalevi Suursoit in 1960 and 1962

Redevelopment of the Pirita track in the early 1960s.

175 cc

Although surviving records (of which in any event there appear to be very few) do not indicate that the Serpukhov factory built a 175 cc racer, it appears to have built at least two.

The vertical cylinder was akin to that of the S-159 but it was not simply a bored-out version of the 125 cc racer, or even just one half of the 350 cc twin cylinder racer (- see below). It measured 64 x 54 mm for 174 cc, and the general dimensions of the engine block were slightly larger than the S-159, to which it was otherwise very similar. It also featured a twin plug head, which was a feature added to the S range in about 1960. (In Tallinn, Soodla also built a 175cc Estonia, but it is not clear whether it was a copy of the 175 cc S or merely used a bored-out 125 cc engine).

Two recent shots of the S-175

An official publicity shot of the dustbin faired S-254.

That these machines were official and not merely the frolic of an enthusiastic mechanic is supported by the fact that, in 1960, a 175 cc category was introduced into Soviet national road racing, for which they were almost certainly designed. Indeed, in that year the Estonian 175 cc title was won by the youthful Juri Randla, who was to be a major player in the Vostok tale over the forthcoming decade.

That at least two such bikes were built is established by the records for the Kalevi Suursoit. In the 1962 edition of the race at Pirita, Valeri Katonin finished third in the 175 cc race on his S, while team mate Nikolai Mikhailov retired.

To distinguish the models from their smaller siblings, they were designated "S-175".

250 cc

S-254

Also produced in 1954 was the twin cylinder S-254, which as the designation suggests was a 250 cc racer. Although the engine's dimensions were those of the Ultra-lightweight version, at 54 x 54 mm, the dohc assembly was governed not by a vertical shaft but by an inclined shaft on the right hand side which ran the inlet camshaft. Drive for the exhaust camshaft was by means of a train of gears driven by a pinion fixed to the left hand end of the inlet camshaft.

A five speed gearbox was employed; the twin carburettors had a shallow downdraught angle; ignition was by coil; the Featherbed-like frame was originally married to Earles type front forks. Dustbin fairings were initially available and small nose fairings were used as the decade progressed.

The bikes appear to have left the factory with silver paintwork on the tank and fairing but they may well have been decorated by the recipient clubs, as those which survive feature a variety of paint schemes - which appear to be the left-overs of paint used on tractors, as ran the (unfounded) joke about the gaudy orange applied by Laverda on its works endurance racers in the 1970s.

Weight was 126 kgs; top speed was 150 km/h thanks to the twin's 23 bhp at 8,200rpm.

S-254 in the Riga Motor Museum

The S-254 appears to have been the most numerous of all the S racers, with records suggesting that sixteen engines were built and perhaps ten complete bikes. It is however difficult to be precise because, as with many factory racers, the bikes were updated and reincarnated in the form of the next model.

The S-254 featured extensively in domestic racing, with leading lights such as Feliks Lepik and Henno Palm being allocated these prized tools, and Yevgeni Makjev taking his bike to runner-up spot at Pirita in 1960.

The engine of the S-254, recently restored.

S-254 engine to the left; S-257 to the right.

S-254 now in private ownership in the UK

S-257

The S-257 was apparently designed in 1957 but it may not have been built until the following year, which may explain why some records describe it as S-258. It was a straightforward update of the S-254. The only major difference was the use of a re-designed head. Still featuring 54 x 54 mm dimensions, the engine was good for 30 bhp at 9,900rpm and top speed was up to 165 km/h.

The records of the Kalevi Suursoit make no mention of the participation of a S-257 and it is likely that only four or five such bikes were built, as they were soon outdated by the S-259 (- see Chapter Three).

***

S-257 in private ownership in the UK, recently restored.

350 cc

S-354

The S-354 was built to the same design as the Lightweight version, but with bore and stroke of 60 x 61 mm, for 348cc, and a four speed gearbox. Power was initially 33 bhp at 8,200 rpm. Weight was 144 kgs and top speed 165 km/h. The duplex cradle frame was described as a cross between Manx Norton and Gold Star BSA.

Wheel size was 16 in; twin leading shoe brakes of about 7 in diameter were housed in full width hubs, front and rear. Earles type forks were fitted in 1954 but telescopics (said to owe something to Triumph design) were used on later versions, and power was increased to 35 bhp. Streamlining consisted of a steering head and tail fairings. It seems that more than a dozen of these bikes were built.

In truth, there is no evidence that the bike was particularly successful; its sole appearance on the leader-board of the Kalevi Suursoit was Gennadi Sartukh's fifth place at Pirita in 1960, on a bike owned by the Leningrad club.

On the international front, in May 1957 an official Serpukhov team headed off to Finland, to participate in the Elaintarha races and the Ruissalo TT. The Elaintarha races were held over a 2 kilometre circuit in the Djurgarden park in Helsinki, the scene of the Finnish GP since the 1930s. (The race was also known as Djurgardsloppet, its Swedish name.) The races, also the scene of sports car events, stopped in 1963 following a fatality.

The Ruissalo TT, held over a tight track through a pine forest in an island off Turku, had started in 1930 and ran through until the early 1970s, by which time local heroes Saarinen and Lansivouri were the stars.

However, the S team's Finnish 1957 venture, with its 350 cc and 500 cc models entrusted to Viktor Kulakov and the up-and-coming Nikolai Sevostianov, was distinctly unsuccessful. Team manager Mashkovsky blamed the poor results on faulty gearing for the tight circuits.

Kulakov was one of the rare breed of Russian rider who had international experience, having ridden the works twin cylinder 500 cc Jawa Z15 in the past. Sevostianov was another Russian who would play his part in the Vostok story in the years to come.

S-358, easily identifiable - no shaft to the dohc assembly.

S-358.

The S-358, being the second generation 350 cc racer, built in 1958, has occasionally been confused with the subsequent 350 cc machine which was simply a Jawa look-alike (being the S-360, see Chapter Three). That confusion may have arisen because it could be the case that the S-358 was also built in co-operation with the Jawa factory.

It is likely that only three or four S-358 bikes were built. However, there exist photographs of this rare bike, and one model survives intact, in the Riga Motor Museum. (Indeed, the museum describes its bike as a S-360, which is plainly incorrect). It is clear that the engine of this bike bears no resemblance to the subsequent Jawa-lookalike S-360 model, which was in effect the third generation 350 cc bike.

The engine of this second generation Junior bike (still at 60 x 61 mm, like its predecessor) featured a revised crankcase, extensive square shaped finning around the head and the shaft had disappeared from the right hand side of the cylinder. Instead the dohc assembly was driven by an internal central shaft (and not a train of gears as was once reported in the British press). The gearbox was a six speeder, power was increased to 40 bhp at 9,850 rpm and top speed was up to 175 km/h.

There is no trace of the S-358 ever having raced outside the USSR.

***

The Riga Motor Museum's S-358 (incorrectly described in the museum as S-360).

500 cc

S-555

As the name suggests, as from 1955 there was also a 500 cc version of the S-254 and S-354. The 500 cc model appears to have been identical to the 350 cc bike, being bored out to 72 x 61 mm, for 498 cc, with power claimed to be 47 bhp at 7,400 rpm and a top speed of 190 km/h.

Probably only five of these bikes were built. There is no record of any noteworthy success either in the USSR or abroad, with its 1957 trip to Finland being the only reported foreign venture.

The chief executive at the Serpukhov Bureau during these years was Ragozhin, the former designer at Izhevsk, but the principal designers of the S series of bikes appear to have been Ivanitsky, the head of the racing programme, and Matusin. But, for inspiration for the next generation of racers, they turned to Czechoslovakia and the Jawa factory.

Difficult to identify but may be Viktor Kulakov on the S-555.

Chapter Three: The Jawa replicas

The Serpukhov factory's second generation middleweight dohc racers, the S-257 and S-358, were consigned to the scrapheap virtually immediately because, in 1957, the Jawa factory had built a 250 cc racer, which carried Franta Stastny to twelfth place in the Lightweight TT on his Mountain course debut. And it was that bike which was to form the basis of the next batch of twin cylinder S racers.

The Jawa factory's designers, like it or not, were compelled to share their efforts with their counterparts in Serpukhov. So it was that the Jawa 250 was re-badged as the S-259, and the 350 cc Jawa was otherwise called, in its Serpukhov guise, the S-360.

(Some caution is required when identifying these machines. First of all, surviving records from Serpukhov appear to be incomplete, and there is some confusion in the numbering of the various S designs; hence, bikes which were probably S-358s have been described as S-259s and S-360s.)

What is undeniable is that there was a considerable degree of interchange between the Serpukhov and Jawa factories when the S-259 and S-360 bikes were designed and built. Although the S racers were supposedly built in Serpukhov, a number of them may well have been built in the Czech factory's raceshop, and at the end of their competitive lives some of them were apparently left in Czechoslovakia. On the other hand, some of the bikes which were badged as Jawa apparently used components "made in the USSR". (Not only were the S engines stamped with the appropriate number, but Cyrillic script appeared on parts of the crankcase and head - and some of those parts were used by Jawa).

The engine's twin overhead camshafts were driven by a vertical bevel shaft placed behind the two cylinders, driving the inlet camshafts and also a horizontal shaft across the top of the engine to drive the exhaust camshafts. Oil was in a deeply finned wet sump. Other features were two valves per cylinder, two 10 mm plugs in each cylinder head, battery-powered coils, Amal carburettors and a six speed gearbox. The engine, with the cylinders inclined at 10 degrees, sat

Factory publicity shot of the S-259

THE JAWA REPLICAS

Feliks Lepik (1) and Endel Kiisa (2) at Pirita in the early 1960s

Sevostianov, Polajev and Kiisa.

in a conventional tubular frame, which came in two versions, a diamond and a featherbed; tyres were 3 x 19 in. and 3.50 x 19 in. front and rear respectively.

Statistics were, for the 248 cc version, bore and stroke of 55 x 52 mm, 38 bhp at 11,500 rpm, weight of 125 kgs and top speed of 190 km/h. The 350 cc Jawa's like details were originally (probably) 59 x 63.6 mm, 46 bhp at 10,300 rpm, 130 kgs and 210 km/h. It is, however, possible that the S-360 began life with dimensions of 62 x 57.6 mm, which bore and stroke were not adopted by the Czech racer until a re-design for the 1963 version. Thanks no doubt to the reluctance of the Eastern Bloc teams to reveal accurate details to Western journalists at the time, such contemporary technical descriptions as there are (as to both Jawa and Serpukhov models) tend to be conflicting so that, with the passage of more than forty years, it is difficult to be definitive in all respects

The Serpukhov factory built five of the S-259 bikes which were initially allocated to the USSR's star riders being Sevostianov, Polajev, Lepik, Kiisa and Randla. Sevostianov and Lepik used their models to win the 250 cc race at the Kalevi Suursoit in 1960 and 1962 respectively.

But when just two of the S-360s were initially available, the five riders were summoned to test sessions near Moscow to determine the lucky recipients, who were to be Sevostianov and Kiisa.

Nikolai Sevostianov was a captain in the Red Army (subsequently rising to become a colonel) and, being a Russian and a member of a Moscow-based club, he was a particular favourite of the hierarchy. (It should be appreciated that Sevostianov was not a career soldier. Notional service in the armed forces was simply the mechanism through which the Soviet state maintained some of the country's elite sportsmen - many of whom took part in sports some of which were, theoretically at least, amateur.)

Endel Kiisa's career was perhaps typical of that of a Soviet sportsman. Born on 1 October 1937 on the island of Hiiumaa in the Baltic Sea, his family had moved to Tallinn in 1938. In 1952, the young Kiisa started a course at a technical college and began to race as soon as he was sixteen. But racing in Estonia embraced all the disciplines: road and ice racing, scrambling, enduro and so on.

He was soon spotted by Feliks Lepik, one of Estonia's leading lights, and he was invited to join the wealthy "Dynamo" club. By 1954, he was representing Estonia in the USSR championship races in which each of the Soviet republics entered teams. Aged sixteen, astride his humble two stroke 125 cc Kovrovec, he finished the 125 cc series in fifth place and was awarded a sports "degree", being the youngest Soviet rider to be awarded the honour.

In 1956, he began three years of military service which, as a sportsman, he was able to pass in the army's sports section. By 1958, he had become an established star, winning the Estonian 125 cc title.

The next major step in his career came when the Soviet state withdrew its financial support from the motorcycle clubs; instead the roubles were sent only to military sports clubs. So Kiisa's Dynamo club's motorcycle section was obliged to shut down and, in 1959, he joined the Kalev sports club.

In 1959, Kiisa moved into the 500 cc class aboard an Izhevsk and participated in the republic's championship races over public roads courses such as Pirita, Parnu, Viljanda and Tartu.

By the time his genuine military service ended, he was one of Estonia's leading racers and was able to become a professional sportsman, sponsored by the state. He was paid as a civil servant and given a state-owned apartment in Tallinn; in exchange, in the winter he raced in scrambles and enduro, and in the summer he had a programme of road racing, using bikes owned and prepared by the Kalev club.

By 1961, the 350 cc Jawa was a serious world championship contender, and Franta Stastny and Gustav Havel finished the season in second and third places in the title table.

And their Soviet counterparts embarked on a modest programme of international competition and publicity. In February 1961, Tass, the Soviet news agency, announced that a Soviet team would compete in the TT, in conjunction with the Jawa squad, with which 125 cc, 250 cc and 350 cc projects were under development. However, a week later it emerged that the Czech factory knew nothing of the Soviet squad's racing plans. True enough, although the Jawa team turned up in the Isle of Man that summer, the Serpukhov factory was never to do so

Nevertheless, the team did venture abroad. In May, Sevostianov was third on a S-360 in the Elaintarha 350 cc races in Helsinki. In July, a featherbed-type framed S-259 was a star of the show in the Soviet Trade Exhibition at Earls Court, London.

The appearance of a number of Soviet bikes at the Exhibition prompted Harry Louis to write a piece entitled "How it is in Russia" in "Motor Cycling" (13 July 1961). He reported that Ufa, capital of Bashkiria, in European Russia, was the centre of Soviet motorcycle racing, with riders there competing for the "Yuri Gagarin" prize.

His article prompted a most unusual letter which was published three weeks later. Written by a Miss Anke-Eve Goldmann from Wiesbaden-Biebrich, Germany, it reported that Ufa was the centre of ice racing but that the real centre

THE JAWA REPLICAS

Endel Kiisa

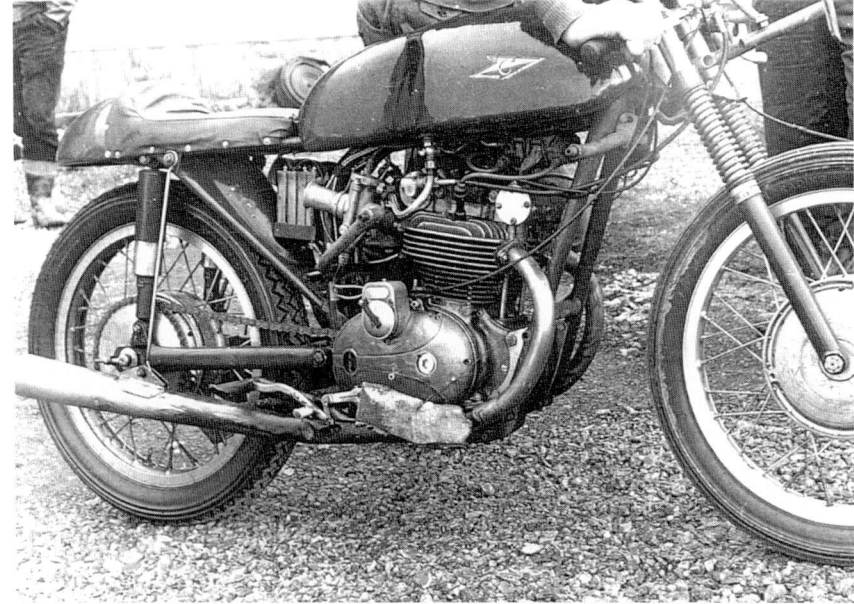

Miroslav Cada's rough looking 350 cc ČKB at the East German GP, 1961 (Mick Woollett)

THE JAWA REPLICAS

Rudi Thalhammer (71, Norton), Ladi Richter (72, Norton), Miroslav Cada (86, CKB) and Frank Perris (64, Norton) at Queckenberg, Sachsenring, 1961 (Mike Jordan archive)

Kiisa (350 cc CKB) at the Elaintarha meeting in Helsinki, in May 1962.

of road racing was "in Estonia, for unaccountable reasons. There is no motorcycle industry in Estonia but apparently the Estonians are a brand of people particularly made for motorcycle racing."

Next, the Czech rider Miroslav Cada was entered on a S-360 (named as a CKB) in the title-counting East German GP at the Sachsenring, but "without troubling the scorers", finishing in sixteenth spot, although he had been circulating as high as seventh at one stage. The use of "CKB", or on occasions "CKEB", was a reference to Serpukhov's Central Construction and Experimental Bureau.

In August, Brno's non-title 250 cc Czech GP was won by Jim Redman on the works Honda four, ahead of Havel and Stastny. But behind them, and ahead of the privateers, were three bikes entered as CKB.

However, the riders of these notionally Soviet steeds were all Czech, namely Pavel Slavicek (4th), Miroslav Cada (5th, and recently the winner of the 350 cc class of the Finnish GP at Tampere on a works Jawa) and Frantisek Helikar (6th). It may be that their bikes were actually from the Jawa factory and simply badged as CKB to satisfy the Soviet overlords.

In the 350 cc race at Brno, Cada brought his CKB home in third place, behind Redman (Honda) and Slavicek (Jawa).

In August 1962, the Soviet riders made their classic debut in the East German GP, with a squad of Sevostianov, Kiisa and Polajev, supplemented by the guest rider Cada. Team leader Sevostianov rode the S-259 to take two points for fifth spot in the 250 cc event; he was sixth aboard the S-360. Later that month, Cada rode a S-360 (again called a CKB) to third place, behind Redman, in the non-title Czech GP (Brno).

For 1963, the Jawa 350 cc engine was re-designed, henceforth boasting 62 x 57.6 mm (which may already have been tried out on the sister machine from the Serpukhov factory, whose records confirm that the S-360 featured bore and stroke of 62 x 57.6 mm at some stage in its career) and four valves per cylinder, with output up to 50 bhp. The Jawa's reliability was seriously prejudiced as the increase in peak revs did nothing for the big-ends but the S was not noticeably failure-prone.

Kiisa on the 250 cc CKB at Sachsenring, East German GP 1962

THE JAWA REPLICAS

Polajev (250 cc CKB) leading Enderlein (MZ) at Badberg, Sachsenring, 1962
(Mike Jordan archive)

Sevostianov (350 cc CKB) pictured at Badberg, Sachsenring, 1962 when he finished in sixth position in the East German GP (Mike Jordan archive)

Jawa and S team coaches, believed to be at Assen in 1963

Juri Randla and Endel Kiisa, probably at the Kalevi Suursoit, Pirita in the early 1960s

A line-up of CKB steeds, possibly at the Ruissalo TT near Turku, Finland, with Kiisa wearing his Kalev club jacket.

THE JAWA REPLICAS

Sevostianov (84) riding to fifth place, 350 cc East German GP 1963, with Lyster (79, Norton)

(Mike Jordan archive)

Kiisa (85, 350 cc CKB) leads the Jawa teamsters Havel (62) and Stastny (61), Sachsenring, 1963

(Mike Jordan archive)

After a fruitless visit to Assen for the Dutch title round, Sevostianov, Kiisa and Juri Randla were entered in the East German GP and the team leader notched a respectable fifth place on the S-360, behind four works machines.

Sevostianov then took sixth place in the 500 cc Finnish GP at Tampere on a bored-out S-360. In the 350 cc GP, he finished in fourth position after an eventful ride. The race was won by Mike Hailwood (MV four) who took a few laps to catch fast-starting Jim Redman (Honda) because, in the words of "Motor Cycle", he got tangled up with Sevostianov.

That entanglement was still fresh in the memory of one journalist who, in a chat show at the Donington Park British GP in 2004, told the story of how Mike the Bike, frustrated by the Russian's blocking tactics, booted him out of the way as an unworthy opponent and continued on his imperious ride on his Italian multi. However, the journalist's belittling of Sevostianov was entirely unjustified; although he was behind Hailwood, Redman and Gunnarsson, he beat three times world champion Luigi Taveri on a works Honda, so the Russian was hardly hanging about.

By 1964, the S-360 was relegated to a back-up machine as the Vostoks took their places on the grids but as usual the 350 cc machines were entered in the Sachsenring round, in the hands of Viktor Pilajev and Juri Randla. In addition, two bikes were bored out so that they were eligible for Sevostianov and Kiisa to ride in the 500 cc event; the former took a decent fourth place, although he was lapped by Hailwood's victorious MV.

At the end of season Finnish GP at Imatra, Kiisa took third step on the podium on the S-360, and he and Sevostianov entered their over-bored CKB twins in the 500 cc event and shot into what was a short-lived lead. Sevostianov finished in fourth place behind Jack Ahearn (Norton) but Kiisa retired.

The career of the S-360 as a contender on the world title scene was over but it was wheeled out from time to time. For instance, throughout the 1960s, a favoured venue of the Serpukhov squad was Nepliget Park, Budapest, scene of the premier Hungarian international race, and of course within the sphere of Soviet influence. The 5 kilometre track, in

Astride S-360 bikes, Sevostianov (27) and Kiisa (28) at Nepliget Park, Budapest, early 1960s

THE JAWA REPLICAS

Juri Randla with Johannes Tomson on the CKB, Pirita in the 1960s

the People's Park in the centre of Budapest, had been the scene of the first Hungarian GP in 1936 when Tazio Nuvolari won in his Alfa Romeo. Motorcycle and sports car racing resumed after the War over a slightly revised circuit, and continued until 1972.

Not only did the likes of Sevostianov, Kiisa and Polajev ride the twin cylinder racers internationally but they were ridden in the Soviet title races (with one bike being ridden by the Italian Alberto Ravaldini). Occasionally they were lent out to favoured non-Soviet riders; for instance, at Nepliget Park, the Hungarian champion Gyorgy Kurucz had a guest appearance and in 1966 the Austrian Rudi Thalhammer was entrusted with a S-360 with which he won the 350cc race.

The final appearance of the S-360 on the world stage came at the 1967 Czech GP when Sevostianov took a distant fourteenth place. Nevertheless, successes of the S-360 continued until the early 1970s when the young Estonian star Lembit Teesalu took it to victory in USSR championship events, winning a 350 cc title.

Teesalu went on to enjoy a fruitful career with over twenty Soviet and Estonian titles to his name. Although he raced in Finland and eastern Europe, at circuits such as Frohburg, Teesalu never ventured to make his reputation in the West. His name may however be known to TT fans, for he was the rider just ahead of Joey Dunlop when the Irish champion crashed his 125 cc Honda, with fatal consequences, at Pirita in 2000.

Despite a heavy crash in 2003 which hospitalised him for some weeks, Teesalu returned to the Estonian tracks in 2004, winning the 250 cc event at the Kalevi Suursoit ahead of riders young enough to be his grandsons.

CKB team-mates Kiisa and Randla

THE JAWA REPLICAS

Kiisa's CKB after a mishap

Juri Randla on a CKB in the 350 cc East German GP, 1964

Chapter Four: The 350 cc Vostok

On 12 April 1961, Soviet air force pilot Yuri Gagarin flew into history when he became the first man into space. Inside the Vostok 1 spacecraft which was launched from Baikonur cosmodrome, Gagarin completed an orbit of the earth in 1 hour 48 minutes; the spacecraft landed in Kazakhstan, although Gagarin parachuted to earth - a detail which the Soviet authorities concealed from the press for many years as it would have deprived the Vostok-Gagarin pairing of a number of internationally recognised records.

With that single feat the Soviets established a clear lead in the space race and dealt a blow from which the Yankees could never recover. True enough, just twenty three days later astronaut Alan Shepherd was launched into space from Cape Canaveral, but it was too late - the Soviets had bragging rights in space; second was merely the first loser.

So it was that the spacecraft's name, Vostok (meaning "east"), achieved a worldwide renown. And the Soviet hierarchy, being keen to exploit its advantage, made use of the brand name wherever possible.

Hence, when the next race bike emerged from Serpukhov, it was duly called Vostok.

* * *

The first appearance of the 350 cc Vostok, at Sachsenring, 1964
(Mick Woollett)

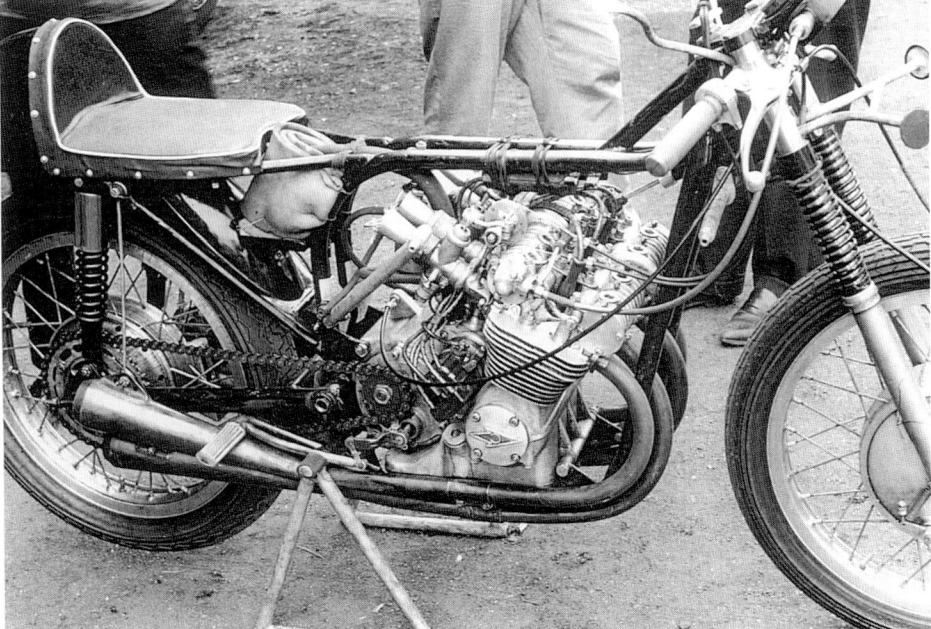

THE 350cc VOSTOK

Endel Kiisa astride the Vostok in its debut GP appearance, Sachsenring, 1964 (Mike Jordan archive)

During the early 1960s, the design team in Serpukhov had not been idle. The principal members of the team included Ivanitsky who had been instrumental in the production of the S series during the 1950s, and Kuznetsov, a director of Vniimotoprom Institute. There was designed and built a four cylinder 350 cc racer, but not a whisper about the project had reached the West. So it was that when, in July 1964, two such bikes were taken to Sachsenring for the East German GP, the world's motorcycling press was taken aback.

Although now entered as a Vostok, the bike was officially designated as the S-364, in keeping with previous practice. The in-line aircooled four cylinder engine, with a central gear driven twin cam assembly, was in the traditional style which had originated with Remor's post-War Gilera and, via the MV multi, had been perfected by the Honda fours.

Bore and stroke were 49 x 46 mm (347 cc) and 59 bhp at 13,000 rpm was claimed - to be taken with a handsome pinch of salt. Other features were the two (subsequently three - and possibly four) valves per cylinder, ignition by magneto and coil, four 30 mm carburettors, a six speed unit gearbox and a dry clutch.

Originally, the Vostoks used the frame and suspension units off the 350 cc Jawa/CKB racers. Weight was 130 kgs and top speed 230 km/h.

The 350 cc race at Sachsenring was actually held on the Saturday afternoon (with the other world title rounds being held on the following day before an enthusiastic crowd of 200,000 souls) and, as expected, Redman's Honda four simply cleared off, leaving Gustav Havel (Jawa) and Bruce Beale (Honda twin) behind him. But Endel Kiisa, on the first of the Vostoks, was next, dicing with Mike Duff (AJS), until ignition trouble put the Estonian out. The same ignition trouble beset Sevostianov, who had been running in seventh place, duelling with Paddy Driver on another Ajay.

The Western press could glean very little from the team. Sidecar passenger, journalist and author Mick Woollett, who was present at Sachsenring and indeed many of the GPs in which the Soviet team participated, in his capacity as sports reporter for one of the weeklies, recalls that the team's shabby vans were always parked away from the centre of activity or attention. Team members who were suspected of being able to speak English chose not to do so.

Lest it be thought that Soviet riders and mechanics were an unusually anti-social and aloof breed of motorcyclist, it may well be that the perpetual presence of a KGB minder had more than a minor influence on their behaviour - as Kiisa in particular was to discover in 1965.

But, just occasionally, the team members would manage to escape the shackles of their custodians. The Italian GP rider Gianni Perrone still laughs at the memory of befriending Sevostianov when the Vostoks came to Monza and taking him to a favoured drinking den in the town for a session which left the pair of them with monumental hangovers.

Although it has often been written that the Vostoks' sole appearance in 1964 was at Sachsenring, the team turned up at Monza in September for the Gran Premio delle Nazioni.

Sevostianov and Kiisa with their mechanics, probably at the Nurburgring, 1965

Kiisa, 350 cc Vostok, believed to be at the Nurburgring, 1965

THE 350cc VOSTOK

Alas, Sevostianov and Kiisa were outsped not only by Redman and Remo Venturi (works Bianchi twin) as may have been expected, but also by Bruce Beale's production Honda twin and Stanislav Malina's over-bored CZ single. However, in the words of "Motor Cycle" magazine, the Soviet fours went well enough until the ignition cried "niet".

In reality, the official explanation of "ignition problems", at both Sachsenring and Monza, disguised the fact that the pistons were disintegrating.

For 1965, the team planned a more extensive assault on the world stage, with a revamped bike. The Jawa frame had been ditched in favour of what was virtual copy of that of a Manx Norton, while the engine had oil coolers mounted in front of the crankcase.

The first venture was to the West German GP held over the 4.8 mile southern loop of the Nurburgring. Travelling to the West was always a problem for the Soviet Bloc riders, as they often had difficulty in crossing borders and they had little currency. But on the team's journey to the circuit in the Eiffel mountains, the problem was that the coach drivers did not have up-to-date road maps and hence got lost. So it was that the squad arrived at the Nurburgring one day late, missing much of practice.

Having ridden just one practice session, Kiisa managed to qualify well, just behind the factory teams of Honda, MV and Jawa. However, the Vostok was difficult to start once the engine was warm and Kiisa was left lagging behind. Notwithstanding a misfire, Kiisa rode through the pack of privateers to finish a respectable fifth.

His efforts had not gone unnoticed and after the meeting he was approached by the Honda management with an invitation to consider riding for the Japanese team. But the immediate difficulty was that, everywhere the Soviet riders travelled in the West, they were accompanied by KGB staff whose job was to ensure that they did not defect - as, in 1961, had Ernst Degner who had ditched his East German passport for West German nationality and had left MZ for Suzuki employment.

So, instead of talking directly to Honda, Kiisa asked his suitors to contact the Soviet government, seeking his services. Of course, the hierarchy would not let him sign up for Honda and a consequence was that ever afterwards the KGB staff kept a very close watch on Kiisa whenever he raced in the West.

From the Nurburgring, Sevostianov, Kiisa and Randla went to the Salzburgring for the non-title Austrian GP. Kiisa had victory within his grasp only to fall with just one kilometre to go; it was the closest the Vostok would come to an international victory in the West. In the middle of July, the team turned up at Sachsenring for the East German title round but both riders were left trailing, with Sevostianov rising to ninth before being struck by gearbox troubles.

Gustav Havel (Jawa) and Kiisa at the East German GP, 1965

Juri Randla with Kiisa's Vostok at Sachsenring, 1965

The 1965 version of the Vostok, photographed at the East German GP   (Mick Woollett)

THE 350cc VOSTOK

The four cylinder, six speed dohc 350 cc engine of the 1965 Vostok …. (Mick Woollett)

…..with an oil cooler added to the front of the crankcase (Mick Woollett)

Kiisa aboard the 350 cc Vostok at Sachsenring, 1965 (Mick Woollett)

THE 350cc VOSTOK

The Soviet version of the transverse four cylinder 350 cc engine, in the traditional Gilera and Honda mode
(Mick Woollett)

Official publicity shot of Nikolai Sevostianov.

A week later at Brno, Sevostianov had the satisfaction of mounting the podium, behind Redman and Derek Woodman (251 cc MZ) but ahead of the Aermacchi team's pairing of Gilberto Milani and Renzo Pasolini.

September 1965 also witnessed two excursions to Monza, one for the GP when Kiisa managed eighth spot. On 26th of the month took place the one-off Italy-USSR match races. Organised by the Automobile Club of Milan, the event featured races for both GP motorcycle racers and single seater Formula 3 cars. The motorcycle races were held over 25 laps of the junior circuit, with each nation represented by six riders, two in each of the 250 cc, 350 cc and 500 cc categories.

The Italian team consisted of mouth-watering array of riders and machinery: Provini (Benelli 250-4), Grassetti (Bianchi 350-2), Venturi (Benelli 250-4), Mandolini (Guzzi 500), G. Milani (Aermacchi 500) and Pasolini (Aermacchi 350).

The home riders filled the first six positions in each of the two races but the Italian press gave honourable mentions to Sevostianov (Vostok 350) and Randla (CKB). But the trip was not simply about sport; it was actually prompted by business imperatives, because Lada and Fiat were negotiating an agreement whereby the Italian company would build a factory in the USSR which would make buses to be badged as Lada.

With that Italian excursion, the international career of the 350 cc Vostok was over. There was one last throw of the dice in 1966. Jawa's star rider Franta Stastny was promised an engine and duly built a new frame to house the Russian multi - but it never arrived.

Kiisa on the 350 cc Vostok, probably at Brno 1965

THE 350cc VOSTOK

Sevostianov (188) and Kiisa (189), 350 cc Vostoks, line up against a Jawa and a couple of Ajays - believed to be Opatija.

350 cc Vostoks at Pirita in the Kalevi Suursoit, mid-1960s

Chapter Five: The 500 cc Vostok

Without any advance publicity, in 1968 the Vostok squad suddenly reappeared at Imatra (just a few kilometres from the Soviet border) for the Finnish GP, now boasting a 500 cc model to challenge Ago's MV triple in the blue riband class.

The model was designated the S-565, indicating that it may have been designed in 1965 (although it had been reported in the press as early as 1964 that a 500 cc model had been under test for some months but was not race ready).

Given the withdrawal of the Hailwood-Honda duo from the world title scene at the end of 1967, it seemed to be inevitable that the Italian idol would simply reel off another unchallenged victory and he duly took station at the head of the procession as the race began. But nobody had read the script to Kiisa who latched onto the Gallarate fire engine and then had the gall to overtake it on the third lap.

Journalist Mick Woollett noted that Ago later admitted that the Vostok could out-accelerate the MV and handled well although it was down on top speed. But, just as the spectators were preparing themselves for an unexpected battle, the curse of ignition trouble beset the unfortunate Estonian and he was out of the fray, leaving Ago to notch another victory. At least Sevostianov salvaged a fourth spot for the team.

The engine had been enlarged to 55 x 52 mm (494 cc) and 80 bhp at 12,400 rpm and a top speed of 250 km/h were claimed. Weight was up to 155 kgs. The bike was virtually identical to its smaller sister, using the duplex tubular frame. But the engine had a few external differences: more fins on the cylinder barrel, a deeper sump and extra finning on the front of the crankcase. The half-litre Vostok used drum brakes but also had available large twin front disc brakes, reputedly developed for (but not used on) the 350 cc vee-four two stroke Jawa.

For 1969, the Vostok was revised slightly; huge drum brakes were fitted, virtually filling the wheel, and a new four valve cylinder head was available. Kiisa and Randla were entered in the East German title round at Sachsenring. Having

Juri Randla and 500 cc Vostok, Sachsenring, 1969 (Mike Jordan archive)

Kiisa examines his Vostok, East German GP, 1969 (Mick Woollett)

Kiisa and Randla's half-litre Vostoks both boasting huge front drum brakes at Sachsenring 1969 …

….and Randla gets a push   (Mike Jordan archive)

Both Kiisa and Randla retired in the very wet 500 cc GP at Sachsenring, 1969 (Mick Woollett)

had to change a plug, Kiisa could manage no better than tenth place. Randla reached third position behind Ago and Karl Auer but he had to give best to Jack Findlay (Linto) when the "four" began misfiring with carburettor trouble and he had to pull into the pits to retire. "Motor Cyclist Illustrated" magazine described the bikes as "improved but dismally unsuccessful".

A week later, the two Estonians retired on the second lap of Brno at the Czech GP and, with that ignominious performance, the brief GP career of the 500 cc Vostok came to an inglorious conclusion. According to Kiisa, there was insufficient money to undertake any development, the engines were worn out and there were no spare parts available.

However, the career of the 500 cc multi was not quite over and on a few occasions it would be wheeled out to race in the USSR. Its final big race win was achieved in the Kalevi Suursoit in 1971 in the hands of Lembit Teesalu.

Kiisa was put out of the East German GP with plug trouble (Mike Jordan archive)

THE 500cc VOSTOK

Agostini (1, MV), Nelson (15, Hannah-Paton), Randla (3, Vostok), Marsovsky (16, Linto) and Ellis (22, Linto) at the start of the 500 cc East German GP
(Mike Jordan archive)

Chapter Six: Postscript

Early in 1971, there was an endeavour to bring a 500 cc Vostok to the UK. The London dealer Fred Wells was the UK importer for Russian motorcycles and in January he flew to Moscow in an attempt to borrow an engine, which he intended to use to attack the world sprint record.

However, the Soviets would not lend him a multi but offered to sell a bike and a spare engine. For sprinting, Wells planned to build his own frame and use a supercharger. In addition, he proposed to enter the road race scene with a top rider aboard a Colin Seeley-built frame.

If the proposed Seeley-Vostok ran successfully, Wells hoped to run a team and perhaps import engines for riders to build them into their own frames. Needless to say, nothing came of the project.

Then, for the best part of twenty years, the S and Vostok racers disappeared, while riders from the Soviet Union rarely ventured to the West.

Lack of finance, which had bedevilled the Vostok campaign, continued to hamper the development of racing in the USSR.

In 1982, FOCA, then the organising body of the Formula One car world championship races and keen to expand behind the Iron Curtain, wrote to the Estonian deputy prime minister, floating the idea of running a title round around the Pirita circuit.

The USSR endured sporting isolation at the time and indeed boycotted the Los Angeles Olympics in 1984. Keen to come in from the cold, in 1985 the power-brokers in Moscow finally decided to spend more than seven million roubles on the project, with a planned new circuit to be called the Tallinnring, to be built on the site of the Pirita roads. The proposal entailed thousands of trees being felled, two new bridges being built over the river, all in an ambitious attempt to build an Estonian version of Spa.

The scrapers and trucks moved in, the construction work began and the new circuit started to take shape. But the finance dried up and the vociferous Green movement became ever more influential, leading to the enterprise foundering in March 1989. Instead, the Communist Bloc's loot was spent on the Hungaroring which still plays host to a round of the four-wheeled world championship.

Despite their relative lack of international experience and their inability to promote themselves on the world stage, there were some high quality riders in the USSR. To the fore were the Estonians, two of whom were Juri Raudsik and Juri Randla junior, the son of the Vostok rider. The pair entered the TT in 1990, and were described in the programme as Russian which would not have gone down too well.

They were armed with Honda RC30s, which were rumoured to feature some works parts thanks to the influence of Moscow. Randla and Raudsik finished the Formula One TT in 47th and 48th places respectively. In the Island, they met public roads specialist John Caffrey and, before he knew it, he and Dave Kerby were taking part in the Kalevi Suursoit at Pirita and the rest of what he discovered was a still-thriving public roads race scene in Eastern Europe.

Soon, thanks to Caffrey's enthusiasm, names famliar to Manx fans were dominating the Kalevi Suursoit's results. Yorkshireman Steve Ward won the 250 cc and Superbike races in 1994. In 1995 an international road race series was instituted consisting of races such as the Ulster GP, the German meeting at Frohburg and Pirita. So it was that Joey Dunlop was enticed to race at Pirita in 1995 and 1997.

And what happened to the Serpukhov-built bikes?

According to factory dictate (in line with Suzuki's practice in the 1960s), all S and Vostok racers should have been destroyed. But, of course, the bikes (and particularly the engines) were far too valuable to be thrown away and some mechanics and managers fortunately ignored their orders. Many of the S racers of the 1950s may well have been broken up, but the engines were saved and put to alternative use - one of the smaller capacity engines was found recently driving a saw.

A few bikes survived intact, primarily in Latvia. The Latvian motorcycle federation's headquarters in Riga housed a small unofficial museum with a number of the S racers and engines, and indeed John Caffrey recalls seeing a 250 cc four cylinder engine, which presumably was part of the Vostok programme which never saw the race track.

There was second small museum at Riga's race track, at Bikernieki, built in the 1960s, just outside the city, near the infamous Bikernieki forests. (The forests were the site of the massacre of over 45,000 Latvian Jews during the period of Nazi occupation (1941-1944). Subsequently, thousands of Latvian partisans (called "forest brothers") hid in the woods until they were finally rounded up, and executed or deported, by the Soviet occupiers in the 1950s.)

POSTSCRIPT

The S-254 (which is now in the Riga Motor Museum) seen during TT week, the Isle of Man, 1989
(Doug Peel collection)

A Vostok in the Isle of Man for the TT Parade, 1989 (Doug Peel collection)

The Vostok engine close up (Doug Peel collection)

Then, in 1989, the Motor Museum opened in Riga (partly financed by Audi), and three S machines found a permanent home there, alongside a range of interesting race machines such as the pre-war 500 cc Husqvarna and the 50 cc two stroke Riga, built in the Latvian capital and ridden in world title races in the 1970s.

Other S motorcycles were undoubtedly acquired by dubious means and their owners have been reluctant to expose them to public gaze - originally for fear of retribution by the Soviet authorities. Even after the Baltic states acquired independence, there remained a suspicion that the Russians would return, which was dispelled only when membership of the European Community was attained.

However, slowly, bikes are emerging. In 1989, four bikes were taken to the Isle of Man for the TT parade by a party of Latvian enthusiasts led by Juris Ramba: 125 cc, 250 cc and 350 cc S models and a Vostok; the S bikes were in the Island for display only, but the Vostok was entered in the parade. Surprisingly, they attracted very little press interest, although the late Brian Woolley mentioned them in his column in "Classic Racer" magazine. He noted in particular the vaguely NSU look of the two smaller machines, and spotted the Italian components on the Vostok - the 35 mm Ceriani front forks, the front brake and the Dell'Orto carburettors.

The first three of those machines remain in the Riga Motor Museum at the time of writing.

The fourth bike, the Vostok, turned up again at the John Surtees-inspired Superprix at Brands Hatch in 1994, and then found a home in the Barber Museum. (Although it was reported to be a 500 cc model, the museum staff discovered that it is the smaller version).

The next machines to emerge were a 125 cc, a 175 cc and two 250 cc S models which found their way to the UK at the turn of the Millennium, and which are in private ownership.

Then, a S-360, which had probably been left in the Jawa factory when its racing days ended, returned, via Germany, to Estonia, where it may form the centrepiece of a proposed museum.

Endel Kiisa believes that there were four complete 350 cc Vostoks and a like number of the 500 cc multis. Examples reputedly survive in Russia, Finland and Latvia.

POSTSCRIPT

Lembit Teesalu (2) at the Kalevi Suursoit, Pirita, with Sevostianov stood next to him. Also on the grid are the Finns, Ilkka Jaakkola (18), winner of three 125 cc races, and Kari Lahtinen (1), victorious in no fewer than ten 250 cc and 350 cc races, at the Kalevi Suursoit in the 1970s.

And what became of the riders?

Sevostianov assumed the role of team manager of the USSR's leading riders when racing both in the USSR and in other Iron Curtain countries, being particularly associated with Lembit Teesalu and Juri Raudsik. He passed away in Russia some years ago.

When the Vostoks were retired from international competition in 1969, Kiisa also called an end to his career. He had recently married Virve Gustel who was a talented sports motorcyclist, having been many times a ladies' champion of Estonia, and their son Marek was born.

Kiisa then returned to college and began a career in business. He still lives and works in Tallinn, rides a Ducati 748 and was voted as Estonia's motorcyclist of the twentieth century in 2000. Most of his trophies are on display in the Estonian national sports museum in Tartu.

Juri Randla continued his association with motorcycling through an involvement in the Vihur motorcycle factory in Tallinn. Included in the Vihur range, in the late 1970s, were Rotax and Yamaha powered 250 cc and 350 cc racers, ridden by the likes of Teesalu, Raudsik and Juri Randla junior (who was sadly killed in a racing accident in Estonia). Randla still lives in Tallinn.

In the thirty-five years since he gave the Vostok its last major race win, Lembit Teesalu has enjoyed a hugely successful career (- see Chapter Three). For good measure, Teesalu also won two car races at the Kalevi Suursoit during the 1970s, being the only competitor to win the event on both two and four wheels. (Car racing ended at the Kalevi Suursoit with the 1978 meeting.)

As this book goes to press, Teesalu is still riding in 250 cc races in Estonia - forming a link with the Vostok tale, which, although not central to the history of motorcycle racing's Golden Era, was nevertheless a fascinating chapter.

Teesalu (63, Vihur Rotax) on the starting grid at the German meeting of Frohburg, 1981   (Mike Jordan archive)

POSTSCRIPT

Sevostianov at Frohburg, 1982, acting as team manager for Lembit Teesalu and Juri Raudsik (Mike Jordan archive).

Lembit Teesalu (21) riding to victory in the 250 cc event at Pirita's Kalevi Suursoit, 2004

Appendix One: Bibliography

Books:

Foreign Racing Motorcycles, by Roy Bacon; 1979. ISBN 0 85429 244 6

Riga and the Automobile, by Edvins Liepins; 1997. ISBN 9984-9178-0-0

Motorversenyek, by Gyorgy Temesvary and Janos Voros, 1999. ISBN 9630390937

100 Years of Czech Motorcycle Sport,
by Vladimir Soucek and Karel Repa; 2004. ISBN 80-902516-8-4

Articles:

The Russian Racers; Motorcycle Enthusiast, December 1986

Russian Missiles; Road Racer, October 1988

Russian Motorcycles; Motorcycle Sport, February 1993

Italian - USSR 1965 match races; Legend Bike, September 1994

Endel Kiisa; Legend Bike, August 2004

The Russian Racers; MCN Sport, Spring 2005

The Estonian TT; Classic Racer, July/August 2005

Appendix Two: The GP Results (points scoring)

1962

East German GP: Sachsenring
250 cc: 5th Sevostianov, CKB
350 cc: 6th Sevostianov, CKB

1963

East German GP: Sachsenring
350 cc: 5th Sevostianov, CKB

Finnish GP: Tampere
350 cc: 4th Sevostianov, CKB
500 cc: 6th Sevostianov, CKB

1964

East German GP: Sachsenring
500 cc: 4th Sevostianov, CKB

Finnish GP: Imatra
350 cc: 3rd Kiisa, CKB
500 cc: 4th Sevostianov, CKB

1965

West German GP: Nurburgring
350 cc: 5th Kiisa, Vostok

Czechoslovak GP: Brno
350 cc: 3rd Sevostianov, Vostok

1968

Finnish GP: Imatra
500 cc: 4th Sevostianov, Vostok

Appendix Three: Where are they now?

1. 125 cc S: one S-154 (S-155) in Riga Motor Museum (engine stamped number 001); one S-154 in private ownership in UK.

2. 175 cc S: one in private ownership in UK (engine stamped number 001).

3. 250 cc S: one S-254 in Riga Motor Museum; one S-254 and one S-257 in private ownership in UK.

4. 350 cc S: one S-358 in Riga Motor Museum; one S-360 in private ownership in Estonia.

5. Vostok: one in the Barber Vintage Motorsports Museum, Birmingham, Alabama, USA; one in private ownership in Latvia; one in private ownership in Russia; one in private ownership in Finland.

The Riga Motor Museum's S-154

S-175 seen at Chimay's international classic meeting, 2003

The Riga Motor Museum's S-254

The Barber Museum's Vostok, seen at the Brands Hatch Superprix, 1994

Poster for the Kalevi Suursoit, June 2004, featuring the current Pirita lap record holder, the Estonian star Hanno Velt. To enter or spectate, contact MTK Kalev, Kloostrimetsa tee 56 A, Tallinn 11913, Estonia. The coastal suburb of Pirita is a ten minute taxi or bus ride from the centre of Tallinn. The circuit's start and finish line and paddock are but a short stroll from Pirita, walking into the pine forest and passing the Joey Dunlop memorial.

Lembit Teesalu featured on the cover of the programme for the Kalevi Suursoit, 4 June 2005.